I'VE NEVER FALLEN OFF MY HORSE

I've Never Fallen Off My Horse

Cowboy Poetry
by
John Doran

Methow Press
Twisp, Washington 98556

© 2024 by John Doran

Published by

Methow Press
P.O. Box 1213, Twisp, WA 98856
http://www.methowpress.com

Printed in the United States of America.

All rights reserved. No part of this publication may be reproduced, stored in a retrieval system, or transmitted in any form or by any means—for example, electronic, photocopy, or recording—without the prior written permission of the publisher. The only exception is brief quotations in printed reviews.

ISBN 13: 979-8-9913567-1-8

Cover wrap image courtesy John Doran. Back cover image of John Doran © William Erickson. Interior sketches © Dan Maiyo. Used by permission.

INTRODUCTION

TWISP IS A SMALL TOWN located in North Central Washington, between the Chelan Sawtooth Wilderness and the Pasayten Wilderness that extends to the Canadian border.

As a second-generation rancher on the Walking "D" Ranch, I grew up working with cattle and horses and eventually began operating an outfitting/packing business.

Thirty years ago, in an effort to keep the ranch viable, I added horse clinics, camps, living history events, trail rides, and driving teams. I also owned and operated the U.S. Cavalry School, where we taught military horsemanship focusing on the era of the mounted trooper. I worked not only with civilians, but with the military as well. This included staff rides, mounted honor guard training, mounted competitions, and equine familiarization for combat teams overseas.

Due to this background, I have been fortunate to work on and have been in several movies and TV shows, and I was the Cavalry Director for the Little Bighorn Battle Reenactment put on by the Crow Indians in Montana. This required providing horses, equipment, and training for the Wild West style show.

I have been an invited performer to the National Cowboy Poetry Gathering several times. At the 2011 gathering, I also put on a backcountry Dutch-oven cooking workshop. As an invited guest, I have also performed at the Northwest Folk Life Festival in Seattle, Washington; The Spirit of the West gathering in Ellensburg, Washington; The Cowpoke Poetry Gathering in California; Town Hall in Seattle, Washington; The Packers' Rendezvous in Winthrop, Washington; and many other shows throughout the West.

Several of my poems have been selected for publication. "Zambo's Dance" has been included in *An Anthology of Contemporary American Narrative Poetry* by Story Line Press. "One More Day" has become a frequently used poem for eulogies.

After my parents passed on, the family decided to put the ranch land into a Conservation Easement and closed down my operation—though I still work with and train horses and mules for mountain and ranch work, and I freelance for other outfits and for the government as needed.

Living on the land and all that this includes is a great resource for story inspiration. My poetry reflects life on the ranch and dealing with livestock on a daily basis—a way of keeping the stories of ranch life and the cowboy way alive.

John Doran
Twisp, Washington

POEMS

I've Never Fallen Off My Horse 1
A Perspective on Luck 4
Bovine Psychology 8
Cry The Home Ranch 10
Are You A Real Cowboy 12
Bill, Boyd, and the Bear 14
Doc's Turned Sixty 18
Eldean Ropes the Deer 21
Enviro Correctness 24
Fence Lines 26
Full Moon in Three Fools Pass 28
Giants 31
Gibson Brothers: A Country Store Classroom 33
Grown Up 35
Down to Elko with Miss Yoplait in the Back 38
He Came To Sell Good Horses 41
It's Okay 44
Coyote 46
Lost Friends 47
Meg 49
Muses On a Cold Winter's Night 52
Riches 55
The City's Cowboy 57
The Cowboy Piper 60
The Packer's Life 63
Shoein' 66
The Circle 69
The Cowboy Packer and the Computer Boys 72
Tim's Nap 74
Wild Heart 78
Winter Love 80
How The Auctioneer Tells It 82
A Modern Cowboy's Traveling Conundrum 85
Koetje's Canvas Casserole 88
A Place of Our Own 90
Take Flight, Wild Heart 92
The Old Cowboy and His Pards 93
Wild Horse 96
Zambo's Dance 99
One More Day 103

I've Never Fallen Off My Horse

Now I've been ridin' horses for...
    well nigh on fifty years.
And when talking with the uninformed
    it's surprising what one hears.

They always want to know the same,
    it's a matter here of course,
To know how many times it's been
    I've fallen off my horse.

Fall off? Did I fall off?
    It begs the story I must say.
But to listen to such questions
    can ruin a cowboy's day.

Well, folks I'm here to witness,
    the truth to you I'll tell.
I've hit the ground hundreds of times,
    but never once did I fell.

Like the time that I was ridin' hard
    way up the canyon face,
Chasin' back a ragin' bull
    up on the neighbor's place.

We hit the rocks full runnin',
    the mare she stumbled down.
I spent three days unconscious
    or just barely comin' round.

But fall off? Did I fall off?
    Sure I had the price to pay.
Still, I was in the saddle
    when the dust had cleared away.

I broke a spur, she lost a shoe,
    I even rearranged my face.
It took us both some time to heal,
    but my dignity stayed in place.

I've ridden out a colt or two,
    you know, breakin', if you will.
And gazed up at swirling clouds
    after taking quite a spill.

But fall off? Never fall off!
    Your question sure does hurt.
That horse he worked overtime
    to put me in the dirt.

Now, chasing cows up in the hills
    amongst the towering pines,
I parted with my saddle,
    been left lying there behind.

And watched the horse go loping off,
    a sight so full of dread.
The cowboy seen a-hoofin' it
    would rather wish he was dead

Than to listen to his pardners
    who would belittle and would chide.
"We hope that you enjoyed the walk,
    but we prefer to ride."

But fall off? Did I fall off?
    I'm sick and tired of that sound.
A low-slung branch took me in the chest,
    left me lying on the ground.

And I can say with certainty,
    more times than I can count,
A fractious colt had prompted me
    to try a quick dismount,

To leave the saddle freely,
    as if it was for me to choose
The better part of valor,
    a planned escape so I don't lose.

But fall off? I did not fall off,
    the ride had run its course.
The decision now to hit the dirt
    Belonged to me and not the horse.

And with hours in the saddle,
    with miles traveled thus,
Contacting terra firma
    is not lightly discussed.

So you can tell by listening
    to my raconteuring one by one
Falling off a horse is something
    that no cowboy's ever done.

Off My Horse

A Perspective on Luck

I was talking to a lady friend,
    I don't recall how it came to be.
But she commented on my risky job,
    and all the hurts that came to me.

And she said she thought in a packer's life
    injuries surely do abound.
But I think it's all in how one looks at life's
    little ups and downs.

Now last season I had one of those days
    when you'd have thought my luck'd run out.
But when I stop and analyze it all,
    luck's not what it's about.

Cuz no matter what seems to go wrong,
    it surely could get worse.
So I'll let you be the judge of it
    as I regale with this verse.

We had just come out of a long pack trip,
    it was hot and we were beat.
We were loading stock into the truck,
    fighting dust and thirst and heat.

Against the headache board I loaded Jug,
    I'd pushed him up there tight.
And next I brought in Tiny Tim,
    I'd forgot they liked to fight.

And as I turned to leave the truck
    to bring another in,
I felt a pain shoot through my leg,
    it hurt from butt to shin.

See, I'd been in the middle
    of a nasty mule exchange.
I'd lost that round, I could barely walk
    and I felt a bit deranged.

But we got them in and tied them off,
    loaded up the pickup truck.
I came round the back, the gate was down,
    and my other knee I struck.

Now the tears they filled my eyes,
    I could not even cuss,
For my leg it was throbbing so,
    now my right knee like to bust.

But somehow we got it all done,
    to the ranch we headed down.
I still had one gauntlet to run
    through our busy tourist town.

And sure enough my luck held
    as I came around the curve.
In the middle of the street there stood
    a sight so damned absurd.

In a red tank top and spandex shorts
    (I let out a muffled groan),
She was three hundred pounds, with a video cam,
    clutching an ice cream cone.

Well, I hit the brakes, grabbed a lower gear,
    kept the words under my breath,
For a sudden stop with a load of mules
    could easily spell death.

But we slipped on by with an inch to spare,
    she thought it all in fun.
I just kept on moving through that town,
    thank God this day is almost done.

I had to yet head to the store
    to provision up for our next trip.
But no danger here, I could limp along,
    use the cart so's not to slip.

Well you may think some grave misfortune
    assailed me in the supermart.
But you're wrong, no mishaps here,
    'cept I left my checkbook in the cart.

This oversight I did not note
    till I'd got back up the road.
And a hay truck was coming in that night,
    I had to pay him for his load.

But he said he understood
    and he'd take me at my word.
So we unloaded hay and I told my tale,
    he just laughed at what he heard.

Well the haying job was almost done
    and the bales were neatly stacked
When someone knocked a wasp nest down
    and the hornets did attack.

Oh, you should have seen the movement then
    and the curses yelled on high.
I cleared the barn and thought I was safe
    till one nailed me above my eye.

Well I hit the trough and dunked my head
    to keep the swelling in its place.
But it was no use, I could feel the pain
    all through the left side of my face.

Now some might think the luck I had
    that day had all been bad.
But if you think of how it might have gone
    you'll see why I was glad.

See, the mule he could have kicked me low
    and a broken leg I'd have.
But he hit me high where through nature's plan
    some extra padding I had.

And just think of where the pain would be
    if the tail gate had not been so low.
Not a bass or baritone's voice you'd hear,
    but maybe a soprano's.

And if that spandexed lady
    had not my big truck spied,
I'd be sitting in the jailhouse now
    charged with vehicular homicide.

Just think if that had come to pass,
    I could not even save my neck.
Cuz if a good Samaritan had not returned my book,
    I could not even write a check.

Then thank God that nasty hornet
    who had mayhem on his mind,
Was a little off, his aim was bad,
    or else I would be blind.

And so you see when people say
    "Your luck that day was wrong!"
I say, "No way, I'm a lucky man,
    just think of how it might have gone!"

Off My Horse

Bovine Psychology

Now there are many ways to train a dog,
    to fetch and guard and heel.
From love, affection or strong words,
    rewards for his pluck and zeal.

And cats they seem to switch the roles,
    most train their masters well.
Aloof indifference, "I own this place."
    All the rest can go to hell.

Whispering seems to be the fad
    when working with your horse.
If you say the right sweet words,
    you know he'll stay the steady course.

I read an article one time
    how trained dolphins save the day.
The Navy uses them with skill
    to keep the enemies at bay.

And over in the hills of France
    where truffles can be found,
They've trained their pigs to sniff them out
    and find them underground.

I don't think that you can train a fowl,
    a chicken's brain, it seems inert.
Still I've seen them hypnotize said birds,
    just leave them lying in the dirt.

Waterfowl that fill the sky,
    when winter's death knell chimes,
Unerringly, with no help from man
    will head for warmer climes.

The sturdy mule, whose stubbornness
 is his foremost trait and pride,
With a little patience and some skill
 can be taught to pack and ride.

But to change a bull calf's priorities,
 set him on the path of life,
We call it bovine psychology...
 and we still use a damned sharp knife.

Cry The Home Ranch

Well, Dad's been gone now nigh on three years,
    and Mom's eighty in the spring.
The house has seen a hundred summers come and go
    and a thousand voices laugh and sing.

And now the torch, it has moved on,
    young hands growing up to meet the task.
Sweet rain bathes the verdant land,
    just like a thousand years in the past.

The sentinel pine, lone up on the distant hill,
    where the ashes years ago were strewn,
Will keep her vigil through storm and sun,
    in the solid dark or pale moon.

The land, it has a spirit,
    we've all rode headlong racing 'cross her face.
And felt the sun dance off the rocks and sage
    as we set a breakneck pace.

But we're now grown and our strength may have waned
    as we pursue our private schemes,
And chase the gods of enterprise,
    building families, fortunes, homes, and dreams.

But still the land, she calls us back,
    and now she beckons, "Tread on me light.
I'm your Mother Earth, I'm part of you,
    I've bled and wept, now hear my plight.

"And though the cattle scarcely graze my hills
    and the homestead sites are fading fast,
I'm still alive and I'm still here,
    I'm the next generation's future, I'm your past.

"Don't turn your back, don't walk away,
    I'm not an old lover used and cast aside.
I'm rebirth in spring and summer's sweet growth,
    fall-colored petticoats, then winter's tide.

"The roots run deep, just look at me,
    yes, I'm scarred, but my heart still fairly burns."
The sons and daughters yet unborn
    of sons and daughters wait, too, for their turns.

We are the custodians, the keepers of the past,
    our decisions will shape the years to come.
Do we turn our backs and walk away?
    Can our actions equal out the final sum?

Well, I don't know, but I'll saddle up
    and ride my pony down the distant ridge.
And talk with God as the sun throws shafts of light
    across the pearl-gray clouds that bridge.

And as ranches die, the cattle herds move off,
    the cowboy and horse are left in the past.
Are we a richer land for the loss of this way?
    Will anything we build now last?

Some measure life in deeds they've done,
    money spent or put away,
Material things that lose their worth
    when measured up on judgment day.

But run the soil through your hands,
    look at the sage and bunch grass growing free.
The ranch will outlive all of time,
    true wealth of generations yet to be.

Those unborn children, future's hope,
    are the answer, Mankind will survive.
This gift we have and can freely give,
    and validate our lives.

Off My Horse

Are You A Real Cowboy

I was passing through the big town,
    back to the ranch I was on my way
When I stopped in at the grocery store
    to get supplies for the next few days.

While walking down the aisles
    with all that food and things to see,
Around the corner comes a little girl,
    she stopped and stared up at me.

Now she must have been about eight years old,
    long golden hair and eyes of blue.
The innocence locked in those eyes
    pierced my heart and soul clean through.

She planted both her feet there,
    the mischievous look in her eyes was coy.
With both hands upon her hips she asked
    "Mister, are you a real cowboy?"

"Well yes I am," I answered back,
    "least that's what I profess to be."
"I see your hats and boots,
    but where's your horse?" she asked of me.

"He's back home on the ranch, hon,
    where all good horses ought to live.
I don't ride him in the grocery store,
    the doors are small and he's much too big."

And these answers seemed to satisfy
    and her eyes sparkled with the thought,
Of horses racing through the sage
    chasing summer days so hot.

Then she gazed up at me standing there,
    I was a hero to her young mind.
For I lived that wild free cowboy life,
    rode the range on a horse so fine.

But it set my mind to wondering
    as I finished up my shopping day.
Do we realize just how we're perceived
    by those we meet along the way?

So for those of us who live this life
    like they did in days gone by,
We've an obligation to uphold the past,
    never let the legend die.

And live our lives accordingly,
    help out our neighbors when we can.
Be an example to the young ones,
    don't be afraid to lend a helping hand.

And partner, if there's a question,
    if it's wrong and others it might annoy,
Just hear those words she asked of me,
    "Mister, are you a real cowboy?"

Bill, Boyd, and the Bear

My young brother William,
    whom we all called Bill,
And his best friend Boyd,
    they had time to kill.

They were strong and were brave
    and prone to the truth,
At fourteen years of age
    in the sweet bloom of youth.

They decided a cabin
    made from trees they'd cut down
Would be a great getaway
    from the distractions of town.

Yet felling of trees,
    they weren't used to work of that sort.
So they used old barn wood
    and flume boards for the sides of their fort.

Soon the cabin was finished,
    a stout, sound edifice.
To celebrate their achievement
    was their greatest wish.

They decided a night out,
    just the two there alone,
Then their strength and their bravery
    to one and all would be shown.

So with blankets and axes,
    and some candles for light,
Some beer stole from the ranch house,
    they were ready for the night.

But the word had got out
    to my other brother and I,
Of this adventure they'd planned
    'neath the wilderness sky.

See we brothers just could not
    leave well enough alone.
So we conspired to scare them,
    no mercy'd be shown.

Then in casual conversation
    this information we gave,
Of a bear we'd seen down there
    these last couple of days.

He seemed sort of cranky,
    more dangerous than most.
The kind that just might attack
    if one got too close.

Then we found the old bear rug,
    one we'd shot near their shack.
With fiendish delight
    we planned the attack.

So Jim wore the bear rug,
    I carried the light.
We snuck down through the forest
    just after midnight.

With rustling and thumping,
    the noise meant to scare,
We'd make them believe
    they were attacked by a bear.

Then we circled the cabin
    in the clearing they'd made.
We growled and we pawed
    in that dark forest glade.

And I snuck up to the cabin
>	and peeked through a crack
While Jim in his bear suit
>	clawed the sides of the shack.

In the flickering light
>	that the candles gave off,
I saw Bill and Boyd
>	standing in just shorts and their socks.

"What's that noise?" whispered Bill,
>	his eyes so wide with fright.
"It's a lion or bear,
>	oh why'd it pick this night?"

And the huffing grew louder,
>	we even rattled the door.
Panicked whispers were heard
>	as we harassed them some more.

Then Boyd turned to Bill,
>	his voice edgy with fear.
"Let's head to the ranch house,
>	and get the hell out of here."

So we took our cue,
>	we just stood back a ways,
Afraid of the axes
>	and the swath they could blaze.

Then we too returned,
>	our mirth hard to contain,
As we sat in the kitchen,
>	a straight face maintained.

And they protested loudly,
>	they were just in for a snack.
It would take more than a bear rug
>	to fake an attack.

Loudly they warned us
>   they were armed with axes and knives.
If a real bear had attacked them,
>   they'd have skinned him alive!

So we all concluded,
>   Yes, they were brave, that's no doubt.
But the jeans they were wearing
>   were both on the inside out!

Doc's Turned Sixty

Well Doc's turned sixty, wouldn't you know,
    it seems hard to believe.
Some bet he'd not make forty,
    but the years they do deceive.

And 60 that's quite a milestone
    when you've lived a life like his.
He never stretches the truth
    when bragging on what he did.

So it is retirement for him now,
    lurking somewhere down the line.
No groveling work and miseries,
    just life's such sweet sublimes.

To ride his faithful saddle mule
    and pack in the mountains high,
Cast a line and drink a few cold beers,
    beneath the summer sky.

But I've seen him as a packer,
    on the ropes he'll pull and jerk.
A trip with him up in the hills
    seems to me a lot like work.

He loves to help pack the mules,
    I know his heart is in it.
Each gets his personalized Vet check,
    two hours and thirty minutes.

Still he's not too bad 'round the cook tent,
    that's if you've lost your sense.
He'll brew the coffee thick and black,
    I now drink tea in self defense.

So fetching water and kindling,
    then chopping a bit of wood.
These tasks most anyone can do,
    at least you'd hope they could.

But he darn near drowned and washed away
    there in the cool clear stream.
It seems his boot slipped on a rock,
    we located him by the screams.

And my first aid kit is getting light
    from the loss of gauze and tape.
See splitting wood and making fires
    is not his piece of cake.

So maybe he'll just stick around town,
    he could help down at the store.
Sweep the steps and change a burnt-out bulb,
    at closing lock the door.

But Patty says he tried that once,
    a bit back down the line.
His desire to help was appreciated,
    but she damn near lost her mind.

The close proximity therein,
    both working in the shop,
Took more than nerves of steel
    and she had to holler stop.

"Go find something to do off somewhere else,
    I beg this of you, please.
You see I have my own planned ways,
    I need some room to breathe."

Now Doc's a good man, there is no doubt,
    his talents they are legion.
Patty hopes he'll busy himself elsewhere,
    she says this is the reason.

Off My Horse

When working 'round the house or shop,
    she's only got one gripe.
See Doc's about as handy there
    as a gopher in a sprinkler pipe.

Eldean Ropes the Deer

He was cowboying down south that year,
    out Cuyamaca way,
Where cactus thorn and manzanita brush
    are the order of the day.

It was late fall and the time was now
    to bring the cattle in,
To ride the brush and oak thickets,
    to beat the northern wind.

He had a brush loop built in his rope,
    ready for the catch.
And riding hard, hunting brushed up steers,
    push them out of every patch.

Then movement caught his eye,
    a flash through thick fall leaves.
He spurred his horse and cut 'em off
    just as slick as you might please.

But then he saw with some surprise
    a buck jump out at him.
Now things moved fast, no time to think,
    his rope flew out on a whim.

And his aim was true, the loop hit its mark
    around the antlered buck.
He dallied fast and backed his horse
    and then ran out of luck.

See, when you put your rope around a calf
    or a big old rangy steer,
The horse and rope will pull him tight,
    the end result is clear.

But no one told the deer about this,
    it's no rodeo arena here.
The deer had moves Eldean had never seen,
    sparked by his wild fear.

He was everywhere he should not have been,
    the rope tight 'round him still.
While horse and rider fought for ground,
    Eldean heading for a spill.

Then the rope got wrapped around the horse's legs,
    then ring-tailed him but good.
And they went down in a cloud of dust,
    the rider dodged the flailing hooves.

The dallied rope slipped off the horn,
    the deer was free at last.
And off he went for parts unknown,
    the rope disappearing fast.

So Eldean learned a lesson,
    though he'd always wished to rope a deer.
Who'd won that fight and came out ahead
    was certainly quite clear.

And he'd lost a damned fine rope that day,
    plus some skin and a patch of hair.
A bit of pride went with the deer,
    as he left him sitting there.

So he dusted off, pulled a few thorns out,
    looked around and found his hat.
Then caught his horse and checked his rig,
    gazed out across the flat.

Ride back to camp and heal his pride
    was all that he could do.
And he felt a hurt that afternoon
    for the rope he lost was new.

So the lesson conveyed to him that day
    was really there quite clear.
No matter how good the chance might seem,
    don't ever rope a deer.

Enviro Correctness

I was sitting back the other night,
    with a whiskey in my hand.
Just thinking of the mortal plight
    of us who live on the land.

Now I could have another job,
    drive a truck or work the mills.
But there's nothing I would rather do
    than work on horseback in these hills.

But what if all these environmentalists
    closed the land down to our tread?
How do they expect the folks on Earth
    to stay alive and still be fed?

And if we all went to gathering things
    like berries, nuts, and fruits,
We'd be okay till the squirrel advocates
    filed their first big lawsuit.

And of course the fishes in the sea
    we'd be not allowed to catch.
Not even crabs and squids and little shrimp,
    all those crustacean things like that.

We'd be forced to live like they did long ago
    in the wilds of the South Seas.
Not hunters, gatherers, or harvesters,
    but more akin to cannibaleeze.

It seems a bit preposterous
    to think of things like that,
But I think it's more ridiculous
    to close a farm down for a rat.

Then when hooves can no longer tread
    upon our sacred public land,
What will the average person do?
    It's too late to make a stand.

But in the halls of government,
    our voice is barely heard,
Cuz enviro-political-correctness
    is today's new great buzzword.

So I guess that all of those who still
    work the soil with their hands,
You know the ones, with sun-burnt skin,
    the real stewards of the land,

Will have to keep plodding on,
    and producing what they will.
And hope that good old common sense
    will prevail upon the Hill.

But me, I just don't have that much faith
    in those elected to that post.
So I'll keep working toward the goal
    where a ranch still makes the most.

And if the lottery I won,
    and to me a million bucks were sent,
I'd just keep working on the land,
    till all of it was spent.

So if by maybe writing such,
    with words we'll have to fight.
It just might make a few heads turn,
    to see how serious is our plight.

Fence Lines

He stopped for just a short rest,
wiping away the late afternoon sweat.
    Fence pliers hot to the touch.

As he sighted down the fence line
it was as if he could see into the past.
    Time dissolving into shimmering heat.

A hundred years ago this fence
was stretched out along section lines.
    Government lines, now in private hands.

First built with cedar post
sunk into rock hard soil.
    Corners anchored with stone.

On the ground too steep for teams and wagons,
mules hauled wire and posts.
    Sturdy backs made for work.

The wires sing away the years, expanding and contracting
as winter cold surrenders to summer heat.
    Notes only God hears.

And merciless time twists the seasons
as the elements eat at the sinews of wire.
    Challenging it to stand.

As always time is the winner,
he is patient, always slowly moving on.
    All will answer to time.

Cedar decays and the wire succumbs to the rust
brought on by winter snow and spring rains.
    Earth cycles no man can stop.

So he sets new posts and strings new wire
in the footsteps of those generations past.
    The new replaces the old.

Where the hills collide, forming draws
that hold the melting snow a few extra days.
    Moisture is jealously guarded.

A few hardy pines took root to husband the water,
trapping this life-giving treasure.
    Aged sentinels standing tall.

Wires once fixed to their trunks now seem to grow
right through the very heart of wood.
    Yardsticks from long gone years.

But the fence still stands and generations have followed
down the line, echoed across this land.
    Man and beast alike.

Earth packed hard and stones worn smooth
from countless hooves beating out life's rhythms.
    Paths along fence lines.

The shadows lengthen as the sun dips down
along the western rim, cooling both land and air.
    Twilight fast approaching.

He climbs back in the saddle, horse and rider
both ready to head for the shelter of home.
    Respite from the day's labor.

Labor that will continue for generations yet to come
 as repairs are constantly made anew.
    Fighting off the ravages of time.

And the wires slowly fade into the dimming light of evening,
like years fade in one's own life.
    Life lived along fence lines.

Full Moon in Three Fools Pass

If one should pursue the packer's life
    and work up in the hills,
The sights and sounds and the encountered scenes
    provide so many thrills.

The lure of nature raw and clear,
    and to heed the mountains' call,
The changes wrought through spring and summer
    and the cool crisp days of fall.

These are feelings strong and great
    as you ride trails high.
Your soul is cleansed and your heart grows wings
    as it takes off to the sky.

But here's a tale of something I've seen,
    it truly was a great surprise.
Cuz who could have known what was around the bend,
    what celestial sight would greet my eyes.

See I was leading out a long pack string,
    eight mules loaded to the max.
So to stop the string for vanity's sake
    would be too much to ask.

And I could not know what I might find
    as I jinked around the bend,
But I'm here to say, my God
    for sure, it was the living end.

See the trail flattens out,
    and there's a stand of lodgepole near the pass.
And a spot to rest your horses,
    let them graze upon the grass.

And rest yourself, go stretch your legs,
    maybe answer nature's call.
But keep in mind the trail's nearby
    if you plan to bare it all.

Let's talk a bit of anatomy,
    but we won't get into it that much.
See, men they have it easy,
    but women have it a little rough.

A guy can just undo his fly,
    then any tree will do the job.
But a-women, well they're just built different.
    This one, she used a log.

Well as I said I was moving fast,
    I'd no idea that she was there.
I came around the corner, it was full in view,
    what can I say but it was bare.

Now she wasn't that small, petite's not the word,
    but I'm not saying she was fat.
I guess you could say it was a big full moon,
    at least from where I sat.

So what could I say, "Hello, ma'am,
    it's a lovely day for a trail ride."
And I kept the mules moving right along,
    my embarrassment hard to hide.

And that full moon it turned bright red,
    a sight I've never seen before.
But an encounter such as I've just described
    was something new for me I'm sure.

Right through the pass I moved along
    with miles yet to go.
Thinking that's the last I'll see of her,
    no one else will need to know.

But fate can deal a funny hand,
    if you're not careful you'll get beat.
Who'd have guessed that on the very next day
    I'd meet her on the street.

She saw me coming down the walk,
    she had a friend on either side.
She could not duck into a store,
    she had nowhere she could hide.

And as I got close her face turned red,
    no doubt she recognized.
Do I cross the street, duck behind a car,
    avert my curious eyes?

Nope, I tip my hat, smile a big grin
    and then I just say hi.
"Mighty fine weather we've got here ma'am,"
    she lets out an embarrassed sigh.

And so I just pass her by,
    I've got to say that woman had class.
See she knew she was the full moon
    that I'd seen in Three Fools Pass.

Giants

I took a trip back to the land
    from whence my ancestors came.
To tread upon the "Old Sod,"
    and to seek out my family name.

And landing there in Dublin,
    we were quick to head to town.
Looking for spots of interest,
    and where music could be found.

It took no time, no time at all,
    to find just such a place.
Where folks stood 'round with twinkling eyes
    and a smile on every face.

But make no mistake my partner and I
    stood out like a sore thumb.
Tall lanky cowboys, boots and all,
    no doubt where we came from.

But the Irish are a friendly race,
    soon there were pints and smiles all around.
With whistles, pipes, and fiddles playing,
    a great cacophony of sound.

And soon the talk was flowing free
    as the whiskey warmed us through.
The talk of home across the sea
    where the mountains kiss the sky of blue.

One smiling fellow walked up to me,
    stopped and looked up at my face.
"I don't mean to be offenden ye,
    yer quite welcome in this place.

"One question I've ta ask ye,
    I'll ask it right off hand.
Are all the cowboys giants
    back there in Yankee land?"

I just laughed and looked down at him,
    scratched my head and thought a bit.
His question took me by surprise,
    I would have never thought of it.

But it seems that folks in other lands
    far across the oceans wide
Perceive the cowboys way out West
    about three times their size.

They see us in the saddle racing
    'cross this wondrous land.
The wind blowing through the horse's mane,
    a lariat in hand.

And maybe in a way
    their perception is quite true.
For we live upon this giant land,
    and we've a giant job to do.

So let this be a lesson,
    we've got to uphold the part.
We all need to remain giants,
    even if only in our hearts.

Gibson Brothers: A Country Store Classroom

Behind the canned goods, down the aisle,
    at the back end of the store,
Stood the butcher's shop with its big cutting block
    and sawdust on the floor.

I found this place by chance
    back when I was just a kid.
Now looking back through all those years
    I'm mighty glad I did.

At the end of the day, just a little while
    before they locked the store up tight,
The old-timers would wander to the back,
    just before the night.

They'd laugh and tell me stories
    about the old times long since gone.
When they were young, so was the town,
    before all these years had come along.

And there would appear a pint of whiskey,
    the bottle wrapped in a sack.
It was passed around from hand to hand
    of those old-timers in the back.

Then the stories they would start to flow,
    they had an audience in me.
So I'd prompt them on, they'd keep the tales good,
    their joy was plain to see.

And I got an education,
    they were teachers in their own right.
Like the tale of a two-day buckboard trip
    just to dance away the night.

Or of hunting trips, and cattle drives,
    and broncos that they rode.
The bottle made its slow revolve,
    a tonic for their souls.

And never once was it passed to me,
    yet I never felt a slight at all.
For I was just a kid and now looking back
    respect them for that call.

Through the misty veil of thirty-odd years,
    how time has passed away.
My mind goes back to the times I spent
    in those long-gone early days.

So when another thirty years go by,
    I can only hope to be
One of those old codgers standing 'round
    telling tales to kids like me.

Grown Up

He was a late fall calf,
    born when the grass was all dried out.
His mama took him up the canyon,
    far from the main ranch house.

I had to find the little brute,
    cuz a Norther brought a blizzard down.
If I didn't get him to the barn,
    this snow would drive him to the ground.

I was ridin' a big red quarter horse,
    Dolly was her name,
Hidabrand stock, from lower Okanogan,
    the rough sage brush flats, was where she came.

She knew more of calves and cows
    than this young kid would ever know.
So I pushed her hard, 'cross the flats
    up through the stinging snow.

Well, we hit their tracks and ran them down,
    but that mama cow she would not quit.
She broke down the canyon, then crossed the bottom
    where the bogs are slick and wet.

But Dolly, well, she knew her stuff,
    she pushed them without rest.
Through the willow brush and the beaver ponds
    with water up to her chest.

And me, I just held on tight
    and did the best that I knew how.
I was soaking wet and froze to the bone,
    but I'd catch that calf and mama cow.

And I've got to say we brought them in,
    but I give the horse credit for our feat.
My lips were blue, I could barely talk
    through the chattering of my teeth.

Now a warm straw bed for this little calf
    would bring him through his first day's plight.
Brush down the mare, give her some extra grain
    for the cold November night.

And me, well I headed to the house,
    its warm lights like a beacon's call.
A shivering wet and cold tired boy
    as snow continued to softly fall.

Then Dad helped me pull off those boots,
    all wet and heavy as stone.
And ordered me into a steaming tub,
    said it would warm me to the bone.

Next a good hot meal and a featherbed,
    I was proud of a job well done.
Dad walked up beside me, handed me a glass
    and said, "You might want to drink this, son."

Well, that glass was filled with liquid fire,
    whiskey of an amber hue.
I'd never had a taste before,
    so there was just one thing to do.

I'd seen it in the movies, cowboys drinkin' whiskey
    when they'd come to town.
So I figured I would do the same,
    I'd knock that whole damn glass full down.

It burned my throat, it stung my eyes,
    it made me want to cry.
But I held the tears, kept my face screwed tight,
    prayed to God I wouldn't die.

Then the glow came slowly over me,
    moved up from toes right to my head.
I felt warm, a good day's work done
    as I lay there in my bed.

And now when I think back on that time,
    the cow, the calf and the dues to pay,
Whether the whiskey or the work, don't know,
    but Dad said I was a man that day.

Down to Elko with Miss Yoplait in the Back

The dawn is barely breaking
    the morning ice is slick and black
Ya know we're heading down to Elko
    with Miss Yoplait in the back

The highway lies before us
    we're anxious to begin
She's sitting in the back seat
    with a toothy canine grin

We've got Ian on the stereo
    he makes the time just fly
Sings about Alberta
    and how "Cowboys Never Cry"

Out across the hay land
    this year's crop is in the stack
And we're heading down to Elko
    with Miss Yoplait in the back

Winding down the river
    man, it's all that we can take
Turn south on highway seventeen
    and on through Moses Lake

The pickup, she is purring
    and everything's just right
It's a cold and blustery morning
    but the sky is blue and bright

We stride on down the Coulee
    then up across the sagebrush flat
Yep, we're heading down to Elko
    with Miss Yoplait in the back

Pour another cup of coffee
    got to keep things running fine
Then right on past Tri-Cities
    and across the next state line

She's staring out the window
    as Hermiston whips by
I wish I knew her thoughts
    with that twinkle in her eye

We'll stop and fuel at Pendleton
    down by the railroad tracks
Cuz we're heading down to Elko
    with Miss Yoplait in the back

We've got to cross the Blues
    and the snow is falling fast
But the plows, they got it open
    as we head through Meechum Pass

Baker City's now behind us
    with cattle herds that never end
We see them on the hillsides
    as we head towards Farewell Bend

We're passing all the big rigs
    there's a Kenworth and a Mack
We're still heading down to Elko
    with Miss Yoplait in the back

We cross the mighty Snake
    her waters rich with foam
Speed right on through Boise
    and on to Mountain Home

Head south through the Owyhees
    our trip is nearly done
We finally hit Nevada
    just before the setting sun

This frosty winter driving
    one just has to have the knack
When you're heading down to Elko
    with Miss Yoplait in the back

Driving up the canyon
    and on through the Wildhorse
The drifts cover the fences
    and the wind is gale force

Across the stormy plateau
    and down the other side
Fifteen hours behind us
    and we'll finish this long ride

The city lights come into view
    our excitement does not slack
Cuz we made it here to Elko
    with Miss Yoplait in the back

He Came To Sell Good Horses

He came to sell good horses,
>there's not a bad one in the bunch.
The bosses shut the home ranch down,
>they claim a money crunch.

So saddle them up, run 'em in,
>this auction's under way.
They're big and tough, sold as sound,
>some bargains here today.

As each horse enters the sale ring,
>riders showing off their traits,
The Cowboy wonders where time went,
>years passing through these gates.

"Give me a bid, let's start this off,
>two thousand dollars, boys let's go!
We got to move this sale along,
>lots of horse here to show.

"He's a big old tough ranch horse,
>just the kind you know can stay,
Let's have a bid, he's next to sell,
>he gets a new home today."

So the geldings move on through the gates
>as each rider brings them in
And pulls them to a sliding halt,
>to the left and right they spin.

But the Cowboy's mind is somewhere else
>as each horse burns a memory deep.
They can move the horses off the range,
>but the past he'll always keep.

And he remembers still the many days
    spent upon their backs so strong,
With rain and sun and winters cold,
    those days are now since gone.

The progress of man is measured now
    in ways we never thought.
The land is far more valuable
    when it's broken into lots.

Yes, progress they say is on the march,
    the Ranch outlived its day.
So break it up, sell it off,
    there's a new way to make it pay.

For the Cowboy and the Ranch Man,
    well, their time has come and gone,
And crushed beneath the weight of change
    as progress rolls along.

So he came to sell good horses,
    Yes, the cavvy is all gone.
He's left to ponder what's ahead,
    to face the uncertain dawn.

He'll find new work, perhaps a change of pace,
    there always is the chance.
But the hurt is deep, the reality,
    he has to leave the ranch.

But those horses... ah, the horses,
    each so different yet the same.
And that hellish word called progress
    is an all-consuming flame.

Yes, progress and the greed of man
    crowds out the cowboy way
And destroys the dream the ranchers built,
    a long lost yesterday.

See, he came to sell good horses,
    the hardest thing he's ever tried.
He turns to leave and walk away
    as a part of him just died.

So goodbye to all the ponies,
    pray God they'll live life well.
As the Cowboy turns the truck toward home
    there's nothing left to tell.

The hollow feeling in his heart,
    a tear slides down his face.
A testimony to a way of life,
    losing ground at a breakneck pace.

Tomorrow is a brand new day,
    horizons yet to find.
A future of uncertainty
    as he leaves the past behind.

Sure, there will be new horses
    and miles yet to ride.
But the drooping of his shoulders
    betrays the brutal lie.

And 40 years of horsemanship
    passed through the sale yard that day,
The twilight of an era...
    requiem for the cowboy way.

And future generations
    witnessing changes roll along,
I doubt they'll find it a better place
    when the horses all are gone.

See, he came to sell good horses...

It's Okay

These words I've heard so many times
    as I've grown from boy to man.
"It's okay son, you're bound to fall,
    it's all in Nature's plan."

So as he'd help me to my feet
    so I could learn to walk some more,
"It's okay to use the hand holds,
    don't stay down there on the floor."

Then soon it's off to school
    to learn to read and write and spell.
"Questioning of teachers is okay,
    just use respect and never yell."

And when learning how to break a colt,
    with all those hours down in the dirt,
"It's okay to spend the time down there,
    but get back on even if it hurts."

We became great hunting partners,
    and how we hunted so.
"You don't need to shoot each one you see,
    it's okay to let some go."

I went off to see the world,
    to countries so strange and far away.
He said to "Have adventures,
    you're young and that's okay."

When our country was so torn by war
    and I was of draft age,
"It's okay to make a stand son,
    I'll back you either way."

And as I held my first-born,
    my head up among the clouds,
He smiled and let me know
    that it's okay to be so proud.

When my body was all broken,
    my career it was now dead,
"It's okay son to feel the pain and loss,
    I've been there myself," he said.

"You'll find a new career,
    a new way to make a stance.
Go ahead and pursue the dreams you want,
    it's okay to take a chance."

Then as he got much older
    and could no longer hunt with me:
"It's okay to get new partners,
    your own sons are the ones to be."

So when my own kids left the nest
    to seek their fortunes on their own,
"It's okay to let them fly," he said,
    "just let them know they have a home."

So as I grew from boy to man,
    I sought his advice from day to day.
Whether I'd heed his words or follow my own,
    he'd let me know it was okay.

See, he was my greatest teacher,
    I think that's safe to say.
And sometimes all I needed to hear
    was that it was okay.

And though it's been so very hard
    to tell my dad good-bye,
The last thing that he taught me
    was that it's okay for me to cry.

COYOTE

High above the valley floor.
    where the rocks are sharp and bare,
he sits on his haunches
    and drinks in the cool night air.

He sings a song of freedom,
    of the wilds and of the night
and bestows his nocturnal hymns
    to a horse-thief moon so bright.

Then it made me think that I was him
    upon that distant hill.
For my spirit soared and my heart found peace
    just to know he's out there still.

And when my days on Earth are done
    and my soul has taken flight,
I'll run those sagebrush hills with him
    and harmonize the night.

We'll make a team, a couple of rogues,
    I'm sure he'll teach me well.
For he knows the secrets Nature holds
    and can cast a trickster's spell.

And his territory knows no bounds,
    like me his heart can fly.
But my body's still a slave to Earth
    and will be till I die.

So brother coyote, run those hills,
    keep looking back toward me.
And deride those so more civilized
    who can't seem to let us be.

Lost Friends

"I've lost my friend,"
    the plaintive cry came softly over the phone.
"My faithful old companion,
    we shared life, and hearth and home.

"She rode with me and was always near.
    My guardian through the years.
Some think me a fool to hurt this way,
    to cry and shed such tears.

"And the loneliness like birds of prey
    tears at one's very soul.
It leaves my heart to face the storm,
    like ships cast upon the shoal."

Good dogs and horses, like good friends,
    we take for granted every day.
Not knowing just how deep the hurt comes
    when they pass away.

The many days we worked and played,
    good partners tossed through life's travails.
Each depending on the other's strengths,
    companionship never fails.

And some folks just don't understand
    the bonds we build with these,
To creatures who are part of us,
    never thinking that they'll leave.

But life's range we ride is not always smooth,
    the trails are far from straight.
With canyons shrouded in the fog of time,
    the mysteries of fate.

The seasonal procession
    that marks out our earth-bound span
Revolves much faster for both horse and dog
    than it does for normal man.

So we are left to ponder fate,
    just how we come to love them so.
How the void can be so deep
    when it comes their time to go.

And though we'll not forget them,
    there'll be others down the line.
Their spirits will stay on with us,
    no more the slave of time.

Then at sunset along the valley's rim,
    when pastel colors rose and gold
Remind us that the body flags
    but our spirits don't grow old,

We'll think of days we've ridden out astride
    the back of our great friends
With never thought of spills or death
    or of how the trail might end.

But end they must, for Earth revolves,
    each spin brings us closer to that day,
Of reckoning with tally sheets,
    rewards, and debts to pay.

So now the magnitude of it all,
    the only truth life really holds,
Burns deep the heart when time runs out,
    and sears the very soul.

For best friends we make along the way,
    when following our life's course.
Might just be a special dog we've known—
    or our favorite saddle horse.

Meg

That day the clouds were hanging
    down along the valley floor.
The cold could cut right through your skin
    and chill you to the core.

Well, we had no choice, we were packing in
    to bring out one of our camps.
We'd put on our extra coats and such
    to fight off the cold and damp.

Now if it were just me, well, I'd probably still complain
    about the wet and cold.
But she was riding with me that day
    and she was just fourteen years old.

And as we crossed at Diamond Creek,
    headed into that old rockslide,
The lightning it was striking down,
    gold flashes 'cross a purple sky.

It had been raining now for hours on end,
    the water pouring from the sky.
No matter how tight you pulled your coat,
    there was no way to stay dry.

We were leading in a string of ten,
    so she was about five back down the line.
I'd look back, see the water streaming off her,
    God! I must have lost my mind.

Why did I let her come along with me?
    I surely could have done the work alone.
But it was too late now, we can't turn back,
    push on, tomorrow we'll be home.

When we stopped near the top of Peeve Pass,
    her lips were turning blue.
Her wet hair plastered 'cross her cheeks,
    she just laughed, what could I do?

And I thought, how could a father
    put a child through such hell?
But she asked to come along, I liked the help,
    now time will only tell.

Then as we broke down through the pass
    coming close up to the camp,
The smoke through the trees gave promise of warmth,
    an escape from the cold and damp.

And down the switchbacks with my shoulders hunched
    we slowly moved along.
And what do I hear but my daughter Meg
    fill the air with a happy song?

I just shake my head and think
    I don't deserve a daughter such as she.
And I wonder where she got all that strength,
    I don't think it came from me.

Then as we stood beside the fire
    and dried off our soaking clothes,
She sang and laughed and broke my heart
    with those bright eyes and cheeks of rose.

For I knew that she was growing up
    and the world was within her grasp.
She'd soon be leaving for parts unknown,
    these days would be the past.

But maybe in the future,
    once she's been around the world a time or two,
She'll come home and say "Dad, let's saddle up,
    I want to ride these hills with you."

And I know that day will come along,
    I hope I measure up,
But I'm on the backside of the turn,
    while life has barely filled her cup.

So it makes me wonder if when I was that young,
    was I so invincible and strong?
Could I slay dragons and climb peaks,
    save the world and do no wrong?

Yeah, I guess I could do all of this,
    at least that's what I thought.
But as we grow a little older
    the past is all our years have brought.

So I think of her on days like these,
    and it makes my heart so glad.
For I know the best of my life
    has been the chance to be her dad.

Muses On a Cold Winter's Night

The moon casts shadows across
    the frozen fields of icy snow,
The mercury is hovering
    near zero.

You look down across the top of the haystack
    as the deer move in,
It's cold... they wish to share
    last season's alfalfa crop.

The horses barely notice, they nuzzle the ground,
    push back the snow.
So hot last summer, who would have
    envisioned such ice?

Their manes encrusted with crystals
    that dance in the moonlight.
Their hooves squeak as they tread
    the snowy yard.

At this late hour the moon is so bright
    that the sky is blue,
Punctuated with stars that kiss the shadow
    of the distant hills.

In the distance, down by the creek,
    the cottonwood groan with the cold.
Ancient sentinels counting time,
    their time, not that of man.

Earlier on, the wind picked up,
    blew drifts up against the barn.
But we're okay this time, not enough snow
    to block the roads or strand the stock.

But the mercury, oh, it's droppin' low,
    no shock if it hits minus 20.
So when morning comes it's dress up warm,
    wool long johns and the extra large Elko rag.

You'll chop the ice and load the hay.
    Damn, you wish you'd done that last night.
But you'll get out to the feed ground,
    no-one will have to go hungry today.

And you gaze out across the frozen fields and hills
    shrouded in a mantle of snow.
What depth, what beauty,
    but like true beauties, be careful.

The pace is slow now, the sun goes down so early,
    more dark now than light.
The place is quiet, so still, tend the fire,
    keep the place warm.

The monotony of winter, should you have taken wages
    and headed for warmer ground?
No, it's your life and spring's around the corner,
    the breakup is just two months out.

Yesterday, when the sun was high, you rode the bottom,
    checked the water at the spring.
The drought has lowered the river,
    it could dry up, but the well's still good.

The gelding's breath exhales in a cloud of vapor,
    he doesn't want to come into the barn.
Knock the ice from his hooves,
    and a bucket of oats, he'll enter now.

Have you noticed how cold the leather is,
    it's stiff, it defies your finger's grip.
But it's warm against the horse's side,
    slip your hands beneath the saddle skirt.

Off My Horse

You've ridden this land so many times,
    the trails you know so well.
Yet in winter the scene has changed,
    when did the trails disappear?

Still you know the way, and the horse,
    well, he'll get ya home, so just ride on.
And your toes are telling you, ya wish ya had those taps,
    next winter, next year.

And there will be a next year, and you'll feed and ride,
    and you'll nurse-maid hungry cows...
You'll stare off 'cross fields on snowy nights,
    and thank God that you got the chance.

Riches

I pushed my pony up the trail,
    past chokecherries and currants growing wild
Looking for the lost herd hiding
    where the cool breeze blows soft and mild.

The cottonwoods have opened up,
    dropping a rain of fleecy down
That floats across the surface of the pond,
    without the slightest sound.

The sun is warm upon my back
    and I'm nodding to the rhythmic beat,
Swaying gently in the saddle
    keeping time with my pony's feet.

Yep, springtime's hit the ranch here
    and every flower is in bloom.
The air is filled with the scent of life
    pushing away the winter's gloom.

So as I ride I look around,
    I can feel the Earth as she spins.
Another year has turned the corner,
    once again new life begins.

And I think of all those folks
    trapped in cities pale and drawn.
Never witnessing the magic
    of a dew-encrusted spiderweb at dawn.

And you know, I'll never count my riches
    in gold or silver that I've earned.
There are more important things in life,
    this truth I've finally learned.

See, in springtime I've got more gold
    from the wild sunflowers growing wide.
And silver hoarfrost crowning tall bunch grass
    on a fall morning's early ride.

And diamonds, have you seen the diamonds
    scattered across a clear night sky,
And nature's operatic music
    of a wild coyote's lonely cry?

Riches, yes I've got riches,
    and I would not trade them for anything.
My bank account is bursting
    with the intrinsic value of all I've seen.

And God has smiled down on me,
    he's put me where I'm supposed to be.
I won't argue with the hands of Fate
    for they're not controlled by me.

So I slap the reins and his ears perk up,
    we've ponies out there somewhere.
And I'll find them on the north end of Heaven
    grazing there without a care.

We'll push them down across the flat,
    and corral them young and old.
And my bank account fills up once more
    with nature's silver and her gold.

The City's Cowboy

Now I grew up on the land,
    the family ranch up in the hills.
I fixed fence and worked with cows and calves,
    broke colts for the thrills.

But ranch life had lost its glow,
    too many hot days working in the sun.
When I left school I wanted more,
    more excitement and more fun.

So I left to go fight fires,
    a smokejumper was my new trade.
It beat ranch work all to hell—
    oh, the money I made.

To step out of that moving plane,
    the wind would toss you like a leaf.
Like an eight second ride on a bucking bull,
    the Earth spins beneath your feet.

And you're snapped up right as the chute fills out,
    senses keyed right to the core.
The adrenaline pumping through your veins,
    you've beat the odds once more.

But odds are odds and when you gamble such
    some day you're made to pay.
And my luck ran out high in the Cascades
    one late October day.

I knew it was bad when I left the plane,
    like a bronc rider who's lost his seat.
The ground was wrong, I was upside down,
    the plane was at my feet.

The earth was rushing towards me,
    like wild horses my chute raced on.
When I hit the trees I heard bone snap,
    and my jumping days were done.

But I healed up that winter,
    by spring I could walk just fine.
So I took a job fighting city fires
    in a town just down the line.

Each day when I would report for work
    I'd check my gear and make it right.
Like a rodeo hand before he rides,
    this could be the night.

I answered that call so many times,
    to the floor that pole I'd slide.
Climb on the back of that big red truck,
    hang on for a wild ride.

And I made that ride, and I fought the fights,
    I beat the clock time and again.
But when you run on luck,
    it might fail you in the end.

Then one night an arsonist's torch
    changed my life like that.
The building blew, I was thrown across the street,
    hit and broke my back.

But I was alive by the grace of God,
    a gift I'll treasure to the end.
And as time went by, the doctors cut and fused,
    but I'll never fight a fire again.

Like a cowboy who's rode one too many broncs,
    and too many times has lost the fight,
I was broken up, my career was done,
    eight times I faced the surgeon's knife.

So I went back to my old home,
> the ranch in that place so grand.
The City's Cowboy, broken now,
> returning to the land.

And I spend my time now riding stock,
> and packing in the mountains high.
But I've slowed down some,
> and I thank the Lord for each day that passes by.

See, the life is good, I've no complaints,
> I savor each and every day.
For I've been to the edge and I've stared at death,
> the price I did not pay.

So the next time that you're in the big town
> and those fire trucks sweep past your side,
Say a prayer of hope that this won't be
> the start of some last ride.

Off My Horse

The Cowboy Piper

Now cowboys are a different breed,
    like diamonds are to coal.
Tough on the outside just to survive,
    but they've got music in their souls.

And every cowboy loves a tune
    and sings one if he can.
And to play an instrument with skill
    is in every cowboy's plan.

See, the guitar and fiddle
    are favorite bunkhouse tools,
And a mandolin thrown in for good
    don't seem to break the rules.

But me, well I'm different,
    some might say a bit deranged,
Cuz I chose an instrument
    with a shape and sound so strange.

I got myself some bagpipes,
    you know those highland pipes of war.
I'd tame those black sticks with a will,
    learn to play by God, I swore.

Now playing pipes is like riding broncs,
    anyone can have a go.
But to see the endeavor to its end
    you stick with it or you get no show.

But have you ever tried to play the pipes?
    I've heard catfights sounding better.
Yet I stuck to it with a will of steel,
    you see, I ain't a quitter.

And I found my life disrupted,
    not all shared my music zeal.
I was banished from the ranch house,
    made to play across the field.

Things around the ranch were changing,
    it weren't the same in my old digs.
The neighbors called the sheriff,
    thought I was torturing pigs.

The ranch dog that we had
    was an old one-eyed blue heeler.
She heard the sound and left for town
    and no one since has seen her.

Then the town sent round a delegation,
    I listened politely to what they'd say.
They offered fifty dollars cold hard cash,
    if I would just not play.

And the alfalfa in the fields
    when the bloom had come around,
They bent their heads back in the dirt
    just to try and block the sound.

The sound emitted from those pipes
    was loud and crude and rough.
The coyotes left for higher ground,
    the competition was too tough.

Then the milk cow she would give no milk,
    the hens refused to lay.
Hell, I thought music soothed the savage beast,
    that's what I've always heard them say.

And the cattle formed protective circles,
    the calves shoved to the middle.
But I kept on practicing those skirling sounds,
    I was getting better, just a little.

So I stuck to it, weathered every storm,
    practiced each and every day,
And after three long months of hellish sound
    the tunes began to play.

Now, some folks think my choice
    is really rather strange.
But I'll bet five bucks you rarely see
    a cowboy piper on the range!

The Packer's Life

"Hup! boys, keep movin' on,
    watch your feet in that last bog.
Let's get through this creek and up the ridge,
    jink around that upturned log."

So you're shifting in the saddle
    looking back down at the string.
By sighting through the mule's ears
    you can check the Decker rings.

And there's a ghost-like haze floating there
    around the pack-string's legs.
As you're pulling down the last few miles
    at the long end of the day.

Well, the packs are all rigged out just right,
    no shifting of the load.
The mules seem to float on a mystic cloud,
    as you drop down toward the road.

It's in a trance they seem to walk,
    it's in line with nose to tail
With a precision turn like they're on a track
    at each switchback on the trail.

You've been moving fast making good time,
    no loose packs to deal with.
The day's been hot, the trail dry,
    but the stock's all sound and fit.

But the day's near done, you're almost out,
    you've got all the night to play.
So you'll hit the town and have a few,
    shake the work off from the day.

You can almost taste that first cool sip
    of your long-awaited draft.
Hear the music of a country band,
    and those pretty girls as they laugh.

So tonight you won't think of time,
    you've earned a few hours fun.
You'll dance and laugh and carry on,
    then chase the morning sun.

Cuz you know that come tomorrow
    you've another load to pack.
Rig the mules and saddle horses,
    then it's back up the mountain track.

But it's a life you really love,
    though the days are hard and long.
See, you're in the palm of Nature's hand,
    you can hear the mountain's song.

And as you move on up the trail
    and the stock's all settled down,
You relax a bit and look around,
    take in the sights and sounds.

In the evening you can watch the stars
    as they kiss the mountain's brow
Where the sky is washed with brilliant jewels,
    diamonds present now.

And if the Northern Lights should choose to flirt
    across the midnight sky
You'll watch the colored light-show dance and shiver
    Before your wondering eyes.

Then dawn will break with sparkling frost
    upon the paintbrush bloom.
The stars will fade, day comes to life,
    you'll be moving on quite soon.

For a packer knows the joys,
    and sights that the city folk don't see.
If the Lord is willing, and your health holds out,
    this is where you'll always be.

You'll ride the hills and work the stock,
    like they did long years ago.
You don't think you could find a better life,
    I agree I think that's so.

And when it's time to settle up your debts,
    and cross that Great Divide,
You'll saddle up, throw one more hitch,
    and through Heaven's Gate you'll ride.

Off My Horse

Shoein'

Now we've all heard the stories
    of the horses from hell.
When shoein' time comes round,
    Oh, the horrors we tell.

Like shoein' ol' Pigeye,
    whom Baxter gave fame.
We've heard the story,
    we'll remember his name.

And the visions of rasps
    flying through the air
Haloed by horseshoes
    and the smell of burned hair,

Snubbed down to the pickup,
    cross-tied to a tree.
Plenty of blood in the air, not from the horse,
    but from me.

But I'd like to tell
    of the ones no one knows,
The ones who just stand there
    while anything goes,

The dozens we've worked with
    who just stand idly by.
No punishing workout,
    they sure ain't Pigeye.

Their names are forgotten,
    they'll soon slip our minds.
Cuz the shoein' went easy,
    the beast way too kind.

Just like an old mare
    you could shoe her so fast.
She'll hold there steady
    as you nip and you rasp.

Yet horses like this one
    who stand all day long
Aren't remembered by poets
    in stories and song.

And I'm here to tell you
    many a horse I have shod.
But I'll take the quiet ones,
    that's the truth here by God.

I've had all the rank ones
    I ever could need.
For story inspiration
    and tall tales to weave.

Just one good ol' blow up
    inspires volumes of verse
With your pards over whiskey,
    as the bruises you nurse.

You can change a name here,
    or a date when it's found,
That the same old horse wreck
    can gain miles of ground.

But I can sure tell you
    that I've found it to be,
The wild ones don't matter
    if there's no one to see.

So give me the c'yuse
    who won't kick, stomp, or bite.
I'm getting too old
    for this horse shoein' fight.

Off My Horse

I'll take all the sweet ones,
    I need no more verse.
Cuz shoein' the rank ones,
    just plain goddamn hurts.

The Circle

It was late October, winter coming on,
    and the hills were dry and brown.
I was riding range, checking gates and fence,
    to see if they were down.

I rode up on an outcrop, got off my horse,
    just stopped to gaze
At the land stretching 'cross the canyon
    to die in the evening haze.

The clouds were roiling south,
    must be a Norther blowing in.
The smell of snow was in the air,
    the sun was low and dim.

I hunched my shoulders, turned my collar up
    to try and stop the cold.
My pony nickered in my ear,
    he could feel the spirits of old.

And the sky was bruised and blackened,
    yet shafts of light cut to the ground,
Casting shadows down the ridgeline,
    sagebrush whispering the sound.

The sound of distant voices,
    long-gone like shifting sand
But still living in the spirits
    of those who rode this land.

The hoof beats in the distance,
    unshod ponies racin' free.
With wild men on their heels,
    coursing through the sagebrush sea.

And the years scattered like wild seed
    as the cattle herds arrived
Pushed by young men seeking dreams,
    a meaning to their lives.

How many went before us,
    their names are lost across the years.
Some stayed to tame the wild land
    watered with their sweat and tears.

Their mark they left across these hills,
    I find them as I ride.
A cabin tumbled, turning back to earth,
    a grave where someone died.

The debris of lives lived long ago,
    discarded like so many dreams.
Iron horseshoes broken like glass,
    blue glass reflecting soft sunbeams.

But still their voices ride the wind,
    so many times I've heard the sigh.
They beckon me to come along
    and follow where they ride.

I climbed back in the saddle,
    turned my pony's head for home.
The jingle of my spurs echoes back,
    I'm not alone.

And I'm not, you know, for they ride with me
    on the wind that brings the snow.
At night the coyotes sing their ancient song,
    as they did so long ago.

The Earth will spin and years will pass,
    I too will turn to dust.
But my spirit will live on in this land,
    in this belief I trust.

A hundred years from now or more,
    a cowboy will ride along.
And stop along the same outcrop,
    the spirit here is strong.

He'll stare off in the distance
    across the hills to snowcapped peaks.
I'll be the wind that stirs the dust
    below his horse's feet.

The clouds will turn that same sky dark,
    like so many times before.
His pony nickers just like mine,
    the circle comes around once more.

And he'll feel the same spirit at this place
    I've often called my own.
With a shiver now he takes up the reins
    and turns his pony's head for home.

The Cowboy Packer and the Computer Boys

I packed in a group of folks,
    they came from over Seattle way.
I swear they spoke good English
    but I had a time with what they'd say.

See, they were talking high-tech lingo,
    you know, computer things like that.
I didn't want to seem too ignorant
    so I joined in with idle chat.

Now I heard them talk of laptops,
    now there's a subject that I know,
Cuz on Saturday night in the old saloon
    the beer and whisky flow.

And if some dance hall cutie
    might take a shine to me,
She might join me at the table
    and my laptop she would be.

They must have been droving cattle
    and a rough time it had to be.
Sure they had some bad old dogies,
    least that's what a hard drive is to me.

When I heard one mention web sites
    it made my skin near crawl.
See, the black widows in our tack room
    have built web sites up and down the wall.

Then one said he had some troubles
    at home in his big house.
I said I'd lend him my old barn cat,
    See, he had troubles with a mouse.

But it made me feel real achin'
    when I heard one of them say
Last night he had a CD ROM,
    hell, that's the only room where they'll let me stay.

But he said he had windows, 95,
    what a sight that's to be seen.
In our bunkhouse we've just got four,
    they're a chore to just keep clean.

And they talked of their stock options,
    they got a lot I heard them say.
My stock options are mighty slim,
    do I feed them oats or feed them hay?

Then one said he logged on the Internet,
    what ever mountain that might be.
So I asked what kind of chain saw he used
    when cuttin' down those trees.

Well they all just stopped and stared at me
    like I was dumb as cheese.
Just shrugged their shoulders
    and went right back to talking computerese.

And I'm here to say their stories that I heard,
    they're rather bland.
So I think I'll stick to cowboying,
    that's something I understand.

So I rode off on my pony
    to contemplate the things to be.
Someone said that Gates was open,
    boys you better close them behind me.

Off My Horse

Tim's Nap

Have you ever tried to reason
    with a mule who's just laid down?
I'm here to say it's quite a job
    if the solution can't be found.

Well, I had the chance one day last year,
    you could say that I was stuck,
Cuz the place he chose to take his nap
    was underneath my truck.

I should take some time to explain
    just why it was this place he chose,
And how it came that under a truck
    was where he did repose.

See, I was loading from a road cut bank,
    I had the side ramp leading down.
I'd just come out from a long drop-trip
    and I was headed back to town.

Well, Tiny Tim was last to load,
    and his name it is not true.
For he weighs in at three quarters of a ton,
    and stands about seventeen-two.

I started to lead him up the ramp,
    we had done this many times.
But with mules you never know for sure
    what mischief's on their mind.

He decided he'd had quite enough,
    he did not want to load.
He takes a high dive off the ramp
    and lands back down on the road.

Then he lays down to take his nap.
    His back's up to the bank.
His butt's against the driving wheels,
    his head's up by the tank.

And he decides he won't stand up,
    he's happy where he lays.
And me I just can't move the beast
    so underneath the truck he stays.

Well, the truck it surely can't back up
    and forward it won't budge.
The mule's the one who has to move,
    I'll just give a little nudge.

So I start the big old diesel up,
    it blows a cloud of smoke.
But Tim he doesn't seem to mind,
    to him it's just a joke.

Then I cram the wheel and I put the truck
    down in its lowest gear,
And try to gently move the wheels
    from up against his rear.

But he only kicks out and lets me know
    he doesn't like those moves.
I climb down from the cab,
    there aren't many options left to choose.

Now a few folks started to gather 'round,
    they've come to help me out.
And others stop to see just what
    the big commotion's all about.

And suggestions now they come left and right
    from folks all gathered 'round.
But none seem to work, we push and prod,
    but Tim's still stretched out on the ground.

Till one says he could maybe move
    his four-by up the slope.
Then we could use his rig to pull
    the mule out with a rope.

Well, this plan seems like it's the one,
    so we'll give it our best.
And I find a big strong cargo strap
    to wrap around this dumb mule's chest.

With the strap in place and the rope pulled tight,
    the four-by pulls ahead,
And we pull that old recumbent mule
    from beneath the horse truck's bed.

Then from the crowd a cheer arose,
    they were glad to see him out.
And the mule he just stood up and stares,
    what's all the fuss about?

He shakes himself, trots up the ramp,
    that's the way it's s'pose' to work.
And over his shoulder he looks back at me
    I swear I see him smirk.

And the four-by driver was so proud,
    he was smiling like a fool.
He's pulled cars and trucks and even busses out,
    but never yet a mule.

I thank him again, climb in the truck,
    it's been a damn long day,
And wave to that most helpful crowd
    as I slowly drive away.

And this goes to show we can never tell
    what just might come around,
When a mule decides that work is done
    and he just wants to lie down.

But Tiny Tim has learned a bit
     and I hope with any luck,
The next time he stops to nap,
     it won't be underneath my truck.

Wild Heart

I spent the last two days on a tractor
    turning earth up to the sun.
Spring has hit the valley now
    and the work is never done.

I wish that you could be here with me
    as life is born anew.
So as I work, the time slips by,
    and my thoughts are all with you.

And the colts are all still fuzzed up,
    but they're shedding mighty fast.
I'll get the fences fixed and the rocks picked up,
    get to breaking them at last.

Then the rough stock all need riding out,
    get them gentled down a bit.
Check their riggin' out, make what repairs I can,
    and make sure that it all fits.

And I'm doing okay working the place alone,
    but my heart is empty still.
I'm tired at the end of day
    and there's a spot left here to fill.

So when evening comes and the work is done
    I'll sit back and rest a spell.
And thank the Lord that I'm blessed to live
    on the land I love so well.

And maybe in the future,
    on the soft wings of a dove.
It'll be you've found your way to me,
    to share with me your love.

For love is a band of wild horses,
    they race across the sagebrush sea.
Elusiveness is what makes them desired,
    as love is for one like me.

But the trick is in the capture,
    how we work them from the start.
For you can mold and train, and they'll be true,
    but you'll never tame their wild heart.

Winter Love

With cornsilk hair, the color of the sun,
    a halo in a summer breeze,
And eyes of blue that could melt your heart
    and put your mind at ease,

He met her on a winter day,
    he was a cowboy traveling light.
They talked of their different lives
    and laughed away the night.

She took him in and showed him love,
    made him feel like he belonged.
So he held her close, looked in her eyes,
    and gave to her a song.

He thought, "She's lost, a frail waif,
    cast adrift on the stormy sea of life."
And she set her dreams for someone like him,
    to be a cowboy's wife.

But with dreams we tend to fantasize
    when they come from deep within.
Still he's only flesh and blood,
    not a dream, but a drifting wind.

Then what could he do, he was lonely too,
    and she had a heart of gold.
So he stayed a while and gave her his love,
    with her tiny hands she'd mold.

But he had to go, like the setting sun
    moving down the mountain's side.
He headed west, back towards the hills
    across the prairie winds.

And the last time he saw her,
    her eyes were filled with tears.
He held her tight, then turned and walked away
    as the minutes turned to years.

Now he wonders, "Is she living free,
    has life to her been kind?
Is she happy loving someone else,
    do I ever cross her mind?"

Then sometimes in the early morn
    as the mist rolls up the draw,
Through the ghostly light he sees her face
    and hears her softly call.

And his pony's ears they stand alert,
    for horses know of spirits, too.
Together they search the distant past,
    and wish for love anew.

But the winter wind blows from the north,
    it's got a cold and stinging bite.
For the little girl with cornsilk hair
    still haunts him in the night.

Still he would not trade the time
    he spent within her sweet embrace.
And for all his days, that will be with him,
    he won't forget her face.

But just as the wildflowers of Summer
    die when Fall gets near,
His Winter love faded away
    when the Spring blooms did appear.

How The Auctioneer Tells It

"Now folks here's a real horse,
    boys ride in the ring.
He's as good as any gelding,
    he can do most anything.

"He's eight years old and healthy,
    I got his papers all right here,
His bloodline is so fancy,
    it goes back a hundred years.

"This horse is real catty
    and has bent a lot of poles.
He's worked a lot of rodeos,
    three-time champion, I'm told.

"They used him on the ranch,
    just like his dam and sire.
He spent three years at branding,
    dragging calves up to the fire.

"So give me a starting bid folks,
    he is the real McCoy,
He'll work as good for a cowgirl
    as any old cowboy.

"Do I hear a thousand dollars?
    We're going to sell this steed,
He's really worth the money,
    don't make me beg or plead.

"Well, eight hundred will do just right
    to open up the bid,
He's really worth the money,
    just hear all the things he did.

"And the paper work here tells me
        he's done all that one could hope,
He stands and clips and shoes easy,
        he's even 'mountain broke.'

"He spent four years leading pack strings
        in the mountains up so high.
He's quiet at the hitch line
        and not even known to shy.

"Do I have a bid now?
        Three hundred, it's a steal.
This horse is everything you've heard,
        he is the real deal.

"Oh, look I just noticed
        these papers here do say
Six years he's led the parade
        on Independence Day.

"And you know he is real cowy,
        he can spin and slide and stop,
Spent time as a doctoring horse
        four years in a big feedlot.

"Ropes he's not afraid of,
        used both as a heeler and a header.
You'll never find a finer horse,
        it just don't get no better.

"Well, thank you now, lady
        for your nice opening bid.
You buy this horse, I tell you
        he can babysit your kid."

Now the bid started climbing
        as they talked of all his traits.
 "They say he's got real bottom,
        he'll even work the gates.

"He'll jump into your trailer
    or the back of your stock truck."
And a phantom bid increased the price
    another hundred bucks.

The bidding kept on climbing;
    the auctioneer was sweating blood.
"Oh, and did I mention
    he spent five years as a stud?

"He's sired many winners,
    their names you'll know quite well.
So give me another bid folks,
    he is the next to sell."

The sale now was moving fast,
    the bids came left and right,
The crowd was now well in the game
    and oh, it was a sight.

But I got to counting all the things
    they say this horse had done,
And by my calculations...
    This eight-year-old was over twenty-one!

And the auctioneer he called it well,
    "The buyer must be wary."
Cuz if you look at things too close
    the end result is scary.

But just as in all parts of life
    you stick awhile you'll see,
That just like at a horse auction,
    there is no guarantee.

A Modern Cowboy's Traveling Conundrum

She called him up and said, "Hey, Pop!
    I just now realized.
You've never been to my new place,
    back East where I reside.

"It's been some time since I've been home
    there on the ranch, you see.
But I can't head that way right now
    so you should visit me.

"I know you don't like traveling much,
    you'd rather stay home on the ranch.
But it's winter time, there's not much work for you
    so Pop, come, take a chance.

"I'll help you with the details,
    I can get your plane ticket online.
I'll meet you at the airport, Dad,
    and things will be just fine."

"Okay," he says. "I guess you're right,
    it has been quite a spell.
I'd love to see the place you live,
    hear you sing, and know you're well."

So dates were set and plans were made,
    back East he soon would go.
A warning though she had to give,
    "Dad, a few things you should know.

"See, travel is not the same
    as the last time you took a flight.
So listen, Pop, some advice I'll give
    so you can do it right.

Off My Horse

"When you're dressing for your trip
    and getting set to go,
Make sure your socks are clean and fresh,
    no holes there in the toe.

"You see, airport security
    will make you remove your boots.
To check for bombs and things like that,
    or anything that shoots.

"And you know, your watch you always wear
    with the cigar blade on the fob?
Best leave it at home or in your bag,
    See, security's on the job.

"And wash your hair, brush it neat,
    make sure your hat is clean.
They'll make you take it off
    and pass it through the X-ray machine.

"Now, that silver flask you like to bring
    to keep the chills away?
Forget it, Dad, see, liquids aren't allowed
    on planes today.

"Your style of shirt, the kind you wear,
    might be a bit deceiving.
The metal snaps all down the front
    will set the detectors screaming.

"Be sure to check the pockets
    on the jeans you wear that day.
You'd be surprised the things you have
    can cause a big delay.

"Castration knives are not allowed,
    they're weapons of destruction.
Don't argue, Dad, you just can't win,
    there's no room for discussion.

"Those kitchen matches that you keep,
    Dad, I surely am not kiddin'.
Leave them home, you can't bring them,
    they're totally forbidden.

"And when they make you take off your belt
    cuz the silver buckle's big and round,
Be sure you've got a good strong hold,
    so your britches don't fall down.

"They'll want to see an ID card
    with a picture of your face
To make sure you don't let another cowboy
    board the plane and take your place.

"That morning eat a big breakfast,
    be sure you get enough.
All you'll get to eat on your flight back East
    is a Coke and stale peanuts.

"Dad, I'm just trying to help advise
    so you can get here.
Be early and prepare to wait,
    you really have no choice there."

"Well, daughter dear, I thank you so,
    but here you are mistaken.
You see, there are still things I could do,
    all options are not taken.

"I've thought it over, yes, my dear,
    and this I will explain.
You see, I've had a change of heart…
    I think I'll take the train."

Koetje's Canvas Casserole

They headed up the trail
    on a warm day in July.
Ten mules loaded down with supplies,
    'neath a clear blue mountain sky.

The crew that day it varied,
    Al the old packer led the string.
And Jeff the rookie rode along
    to learn a bit of everything.

But the stranger there on this first trip,
    with a smile so big and wide,
Was Paul Koetje, a fisherman
    and buddy from the Other Side.

He rode to help the boys there
    and enjoy the mountains grand,
To learn a little of the trade
    and lend a helping hand.

So when they hit the old camp spot
    the cook tent was put right.
Al and Jeff worked with the gear and stock
    while Koetje set the stove alight.

He got a fire blazing
    in the blackened old wood stove.
But he forgot to check the oven
    and remove what it might hold.

See, Al had placed a tarp in there
    to keep the rack quiet.
You'd think that one might check this out
    before he tried to light it.

So as the temp it started rising,
    the contents began to bake.
Smoke filled the tent and billowed out,
    here are the steps they'd take.

Al grabbed an axe and water jug,
    Jeff was there with one quick shout.
They removed the burning canvas,
    then they stomped the fire out.

When they'd finished with the smoldering mess,
    it left the tent a smoky hue.
They ribbed poor Kutch unmercifully,
    as cowboys are wont to do.

Al said, "I hate to quiz the cook,
    but this smoke is in my eye.
If I stay much longer in this tent,
    I'm surely going to die."

But Koetje touted its healthfulness,
    he proclaimed to one and all.
It was very high in fiber
    and had no cholesterol.

Still the boys they grumbled loudly
    as they passed the bottle around.
"Koetje, if you're going to cook this trip
    we're headed back to town."

They cleaned the tent, rustled up some grub,
    it satisfied body, mind and soul.
But the joke around the camp that year
    was Koetje's canvas casserole.

A Place of Our Own

I know that times are a little lean,
    they been this way a while.
I guess that being on the land
    ain't livin' life in style.

This old house is bent and weather-worn,
    it rattles in a blow.
A little cramped for the likes of us,
    no room left here to grow.

Yet I know that you're still happy
    and you've made the place a home.
But I see it in your eyes at times,
    when your thoughts begin to roam.

And I know that you may not be aware
    of how I plot and scheme
In the early hours as by your side
    my heart fills with the dream

Of the way that we might make ends meet
    and put a little away
To have for our own special place
    we're bound to find someday.

I know it well in my own mind,
    and we've laughed and talked of such,
Where we can stand on our own land,
    we really don't ask much.

Some ground where we can run the cows,
    just enough to make a go.
A patch of earth beside the barn
    where your garden it can grow.

A cottonwood standing tall there
    by the front yard gate.
With a swing for the kids, and the promise of shade
    when the day grows hot and late.

And on the porch a couple of chairs
    where some peace we just might find.
I'll pick out your star from Heaven above
    and you can point out mine.

Both you and I are neither one afraid
    of the work such a place might hold.
Our hopes and dreams, what we ask of life,
    don't amount to much, all told.

A horse and saddle fit for our needs,
    so that we can ride all day
Across the sage and bunch grass covered hills,
    up the ridge where pine trees sway.

And someday yes, we'll have all of this,
    for hard work makes the dream come true.
See God smiles upon the endeavors
    of the likes of me and you.

So Hon, don't be discouraged
    when the day's work piles up so high
Cuz we're a team and if we pull as one,
    we'll get there by and by.

Take Flight, Wild Heart

Take flight wild heart across the sky,
    and soar on eagles' wings
Amidst the clouds' surreal lace,
    past the place where angels sing.

Take flight wild heart, shake off the bounds of Earth,
    leave behind the bright green sod.
Throw caution out, defy the decrees of Man
    and kiss the cheek of God.

Take flight wild heart, aim for the stars,
    no fetters to constrain.
For with love to lift you on the wings of joy,
    your greatest dreams you can obtain.

Take flight wild heart, glide past the sun,
    cast not your shadow on the Earth
And ride the wind past your old fears
    to witness love's rebirth.

Take flight wild heart, leave your fortress soul
    and begin your life anew.
Then gamble on a lover's dream,
    before your life is through.

Take flight wild heart, set a course towards me,
    though the path be fraught with stones.
For in the end, when it's come to pass,
    this life you lead is still your own.

Take flight wild heart, though the journey's long
    my light will lead the way.
Then rest and shelter in my loving arms,
    forever and a day.

The Old Cowboy and His Pards

I hadn't noticed the old cowboy,
    but I was just a kid.
We were at an auction out of town,
    I watched Dad's every bid.

He was bidding on a quarter horse mare,
    Oh, she was a handsome sight—
Red sorrel and four stockinged feet,
    eyes intelligent and bright.

With Dad's winning bid the crowd moved on,
    but I stayed to brush her down.
That's when I saw the old cowboy
    just sort of hanging around.

So I walked up to the old timer,
    he looked like he had a yarn to tell
With a two-day beard, his hat stained throughout,
    but from his eyes the laughter fell.

And he asked, "Where you from, son?
    I see your dad he bought the mare.
She comes from a good old bloodline,
    the two of you will make a pair."

I said that I was from up at Twisp,
    a ranch just out of town a ways.
"Twisp!" he says. "I know it well,
    I cowboyed there in my younger days."

And his eyes they sparkled brighter now
    as his stories came to life.
Stories of cattle drives and rodeos
    and how he met his wife.

He said, "You know I'm not ashamed
    to say at times I drink a bit.
And is your place the one north of town
    where the slaughterhouse did sit?"

I said, "Yes, that's the one,
    where the old stage used to run."
He laughed out loud and softly said,
    "I'd like to tell you something, son.

"When the law made whiskey hard to find
    and saloons were all shut down
The cowboys had to use their wits
    when they headed into town.

"And if you knew the right folks,
    and you used your head to think
There were ways a thirsty cowboy
    could find something to drink.

"Just outside of town,
    on the place you described to me,
Was an old milk can like the creamery used
    hidden just behind a tree.

"If you left an old quart mason jar
    and a dollar bill or two
When you came back in a short time
    the jar was filled with mountain dew."

And he described to me in detail
    that milk can's hiding place.
He said, "When you get home go check out there,
    still might be a trace."

So I did just as he said
    to see what might be found
And sure enough the milk can
    lay rusting on the ground.

I brushed the dirt and leaves away,
    hauled it out and checked inside.
Nope, no whiskey jar,
    but the cowboy had not lied.

And now so many odd years gone,
    and I look back upon that day
I conjure up a scene from there
    and the waning cowboy way.

I don't know his name and never saw him again
    in all these bygone days
But he's alive with all his pards,
    and in my mind that's where he'll stay.

And that moonshine still that once produced
    up above the high water line
Is left to fade away
    in the eternal fog of time.

Wild Horse

Out there still unbranded,
    you're wild and running free.
You dark old rangy cayuse,
    you're an awful lot like me.

And memories are treasures
    that we keep well packed away
To bring back to the surface
    on those snowy winter days.

Yes, the memories of our youth
    when we were still so strong,
Living our life fully
    and the days were warm and long.

With scars along your flanks now,
    oh, what fights these had to be.
You wild old freedom-loving cuss,
    you're an awful lot like me.

I bet your knees begin to ache
    when the air turns crisp and raw.
And Northers whip the pine-clad hills
    and howl down through the draw.

You turn your back into the wind,
    your resolve not dimmed by age.
How many years we've played out our roles
    upon life's shifting stage.

And seek the warmer hollows,
    the mountain's sheltered lee.
You scarred old tough caballo,
    you're an awful lot like me.

You've had your run with mares so fine,
    you led them with a will,
Fought off attacks from young upstarts
    with courage, strength, and skill.

The bloodline has not ceased to be,
    the offspring keep it alive.
They'll pass along your wild skills
    and assure they will survive.

You keep them out of harm's way,
    your task so plain to see.
You wise and brave old patriarch,
    you're an awful lot like me.

Through years of drought and fire,
    when feed was mostly gone,
You led them to northern slopes
    where grasses still grew long.

When winter snows and blizzards
    made the feeding oh-so-rough,
It's to the wind-swept ridge you went,
    where they might get just enough.

You made sure that none went hungry,
    though your ribs they all could see.
You unswerving old provider,
    you're an awful lot like me.

When pushed to leave your beloved land,
    where you've been so free to roam,
You'd make a stand with unbridled strength,
    to save what you call home.

And safety was so paramount,
    for this band you bravely led,
The enemies you'd keep at bay,
    till all had safely fled.

You fought with the convictions of your kind,
    against all the powers that be.
You cagey old reclusive beast,
    you're an awful lot like me.

And held onto your freedoms,
    though the run sometimes was long,
You weathered all the cuts of time,
    but your youth is long-since gone.

You live a life well past your prime,
    your twilight years are near,
The parallels between us show
    there is nothing left to fear.

You wish to finish out your years,
    unfenced upon the sagebrush sea.
You tired, proud old wild horse,
    you're an awful lot like me.

Zambo's Dance

I was packing in a hunting camp
    on a wet and nasty day.
My hat pulled down against the cold,
    it was snowing most the way.

Now the lead horse I was riding
    had not been long in my string.
With little time in the mountains
    he would shy at most anything.

I was leading 'bout a dozen head
    and this new horse wasn't sure.
He saw rock monsters at every turn,
    jumped at each new sound he heard.

But we got to camp and set it up
    in a clearing with lodgepole pine.
There was lots of wood, the creek ran clear,
    so the boys would be just fine.

So this green lead horse was resting quiet,
    munching grass along the trail.
'Round the horn the first mule's lead I'd thrown
    as the others I pigtailed.

Well, I guess those monsters came to life
    when I was six mules down
For the lead horse bucked, he kicked and broke
    then headed back towards town.

And the first mule had his rope wrapped tight,
    he'd no choice but to run.
While the third one back he braced his feet,
    the pigtail went like a gun.

Well, the hounds of hell were at him now,
    he knew that death was near.
So down the trail he runs throwing mud and snow
    with bulged eyes showing off his fear.

No way I'd catch that horse on foot,
    it'd be useless for to try.
So I jumped in the saddle of a client horse,
    went at him on the fly.

We passed them on a wide turn,
    about half a mile down the trail.
I turned my horse, let him block their path
    and stopped them with no fail.

Now the horse I rode was all run out,
    he was blown and streaked with sweat.
He hadn't planned to work that hard,
    that's all the run from him I'd get.

So I jumped back up on Zambo's back,
    he's the one who'd run away.
I figured he had strength enough
    to finish out this day.

But once again the hounds of hell
    have gone on the attack.
So in a panic run he backed up the trail,
    but this time with me on his back.

Now he's got no reins, no headstall at all,
    just a lead rope for my grip.
And at each bound now he puts on more speed,
    I just know he's going to trip.

Then he heads in for the lodgepole,
    to the jim-jam dead and old.
Hell! He'll kill us both when he hits the logs,
    I've got to get control.

So I pull the old Colt .45
    that's been strapped to my side.
I don't mean to shoot, just rap him once,
    a drastic step to save my hide.

But as my hand comes down, his head rears up,
    I was aiming for his pole,
And the combined forces meeting thus,
    they really take their toll.

His lights went out like I'd pulled the switch,
    and he buckled at the knee.
We cartwheeled once, I threw out my arms
    as the ground rushed up at me.

Now the .45 held in my grip,
    I could not just let go.
It's an heirloom from my dad,
    who's had it 70 years or so.

So with arms outstretched I hit the ground,
    rolled in the snow and mud,
And the pistol hit me in the head,
    you should have seen the blood.

Well, the horse and I disentangled there
    and he stood and shook his head.
While my clients all came rushing down,
    would their packer soon be dead?

So I stood up and staunched the flow
    of blood running down my face,
and the boys they gave a collective sigh,
    guess I'd been put in my place.

Then they handed me a whiskey glass,
    they had filled it all the way.
Said, "Drink this down, take every drop
    before you hear what we've to say.

Off My Horse

"You see, we liked your little show,
    it was grand we do declare.
But our cameras all were packed away
    in the tent with all the gear.

"So if you would just one more time
    take your horse through that same fall,
So we could have another chance
    to get a picture of it all?"

Well, it took a bit for this to sink in,
    what it really was they asked.
They liked it so much an extra fifty bucks I charged,
    as entertainment tax.

But their request I did decline,
    we'd both had quite enough.
Yet I'm sure the guys from out of town
    think the cowboys here are tough.

And you probably wonder about the horse,
    would I keep him in the string?
Or take him to the sale yard
    and sell him in the spring?

Well I kept him on, I thought it fair
    to give him one more chance
Cuz I'm part to blame, I know that's true,
    so he'll stay here on the ranch.

But we've learned some from our mistakes,
    of this I have no doubt.
But I ride him now with a stout tie-down
    and a spade bit in his mouth.

And we're getting along, we're doing fine,
    we've covered lots of ground.
Still I never pull that pistol out
    while that pony's hangin' 'round.